797,885 Books

are available to read at

www.ForgottenBooks.com

Forgotten Books' App
Available for mobile, tablet & eReader

ISBN 978-1-333-68940-7
PIBN 10536027

This book is a reproduction of an important historical work. Forgotten Books uses
state-of-the-art technology to digitally reconstruct the work, preserving the original format
whilst repairing imperfections present in the aged copy. In rare cases, an imperfection in
the original, such as a blemish or missing page, may be replicated in our edition. We do,
however, repair the vast majority of imperfections successfully; any imperfections that
remain are intentionally left to preserve the state of such historical works.

1 MONTH OF
FREE
READING

at

www.ForgottenBooks.com

By purchasing this book you are
eligible for one month membership to
ForgottenBooks.com, giving you
unlimited access to our entire
collection of over 700,000 titles via
our web site and mobile apps.

To claim your free month visit:

www.forgottenbooks.com/free536027

English
Français
Deutsche
Italiano
Español
Português

www.forgottenbooks.com

Mythology Photography **Fiction**
Fishing Christianity **Art** Cooking
Essays Buddhism Freemasonry
Medicine **Biology** Music **Ancient
Egypt** Evolution Carpentry Physics
Dance Geology **Mathematics** Fitness
Shakespeare **Folklore** Yoga Marketing
Confidence Immortality Biographies
Poetry **Psychology** Witchcraft
Electronics Chemistry History **Law**
Accounting **Philosophy** Anthropology
Alchemy Drama Quantum Mechanics
Atheism Sexual Health **Ancient History**
Entrepreneurship Languages Sport
Paleontology Needlework Islam
Metaphysics Investment Archaeology
Parenting Statistics Criminology
Motivational

NOTES OF COLONEL W. G. MOORE, PRIVATE SECRETARY TO PRESIDENT JOHNSON, 1866-1868

CONTRIBUTED BY

ST. GEORGE L. SIOUSSAT

REPRINTED FROM THE

American Historical Review

VOL. XIX., NO. 1   OCTOBER, 1913

[Reprinted from THE AMERICAN HISTORICAL REVIEW, Vol. XIX., No. 1, Oct., 1913.]

DOCUMENTS

Notes of Colonel W. G. Moore, Private Secretary to President Johnson, 1866–1868

[The introduction to these notes is contributed by Professor St. George L. Sioussat of Vanderbilt University, to whom we are also indebted for procuring the text. The annotations have been supplied by the managing editor, with some aid from Professor Sioussat. A reference to Colonel Moore's intimate knowledge of President Johnson's affairs, especially at the time of the impeachment trial, and apparently also a reference to this private record, may be seen in S. S. Cox's *Three Decades of Federal Legislation*, p. 591.]

WILLIAM GEORGE MOORE, the compiler of these "Notes", was born November 30, 1829, and died July 22, 1898. He served as a private, corporal, and sergeant in the National Rifles, District of Columbia Volunteers, April 15 to July 15, 1861. From May 1, 1865, to November 5, 1866, he was assistant adjutant-general of volunteers, with the rank of major. November 14, 1866, he was appointed paymaster with the rank of major, but his testimony at the impeachment trial showed that his real function was that of private secretary to the President. December 2, 1865, he was commissioned brevet lieutenant-colonel and colonel of volunteers, and March 2, 1867, lieutenant-colonel in the U. S. Army, for faithful and meritorious service. He resigned April 12, 1870. In December, 1886, he was appointed major and superintendent of police of the District of Columbia and he retained this office until the time of his death.

In the impeachment proceedings he was summoned by the prosecution to testify as to his correction of a report of one of the President's speeches; and by the defense to give evidence in the matter of the delivery of Thomas Ewing's nomination as Secretary of War.

Colonel Moore enjoyed the entire confidence of President Johnson. According to his own testimony, his service as secretary began in November, 1865. An expert stenographer, he made use of the opportunities which his position afforded him to take down, in shorthand, remarks and conversations which seemed of interest and importance. The "Notes" which follow were transcribed by him, apparently during the impeachment proceedings, in his own (long) hand. The volume in which they are contained—a bound diary or journal book of 1868—is among the papers of President Johnson which remain in the possession of Hon. A. J. Patterson, of Greenville, Tennessee, a grandson of President Johnson, who has kindly consented to their publication.

It may be added that most of the originals of the letters, scrapbooks, etc., to which reference is made in the "Notes", are now among the Johnson Manuscripts in the Library of Congress.

St. George L. Sioussat.

May 7, 1867. { Secy Stanton, and Jeff. Davis.

At Cabinet meeting today Secretary Stanton submitted, with an endorsement "Respy referred to the President for his instructions", a letter addressed to the War Dept. by L. H. Chandler, U. S. Dist. Atty. for Va., dated Norfolk, May 4, 1867, requesting "an order upon the Commandant at Fortress Monroe, directing him to surrender Jefferson Davis to the U. S. Marshal or his deputies, upon any process which may issue from the Federal Court." The President asked, "Well, Mr. Secretary, what recommendation have you to make in this case?" The Secretary: "I have no recommendation to make." The President thereupon directed that the application should be "returned to the Honble the Secretary of War, who will at once issue the order requested by District Attorney Chandler."[1]

The President narrated the above incident as illustrative of the manner in which the Secretary avoided responsibility.

October, 1866. { Mexican Mission and Genl. Grant.

The Cabinet had for some time had under consideration the question of the occupation of Mexico by the military forces of the French. It was finally determined that definite instructions should be given to Lewis D. Campbell,[2] who had been some time before appointed Minister to Mexico, but had been prevented from proceeding to that country by its disturbed condition. Upon the President's own suggestion, it was decided that, in order that *prestige* might be given to his mission, he should proceed in a war vessel and be accompanied by General Grant. This arrangement, however, was defeated by the General, who, although he had been consulted upon the subject by the President, and when he had urged that he desired to be in Washington upon the assembling of Congress,[3] had been told that he could easily do so, (the moral influence of his presence with our Minister and his advice being all that was desired,) declined to receive instructions from the Secretary of State at the hands of Mr. Campbell, alleging that being in the military service of the U. S., he was not subject to orders from the State Dept. The letter of Secretary Seward, however, expressly stated, "*By direction of the President,* I request you to proceed to Mexico, or its vicinity, to act in concert there with and as an adviser of Lewis D. Campbell, Esqr. Minister Plenipotentiary of the U. S. to the Republic of Mexico." Mr. Seward's letter bore date Oct. 20, 1866.

[1] The order, dated May 8, and in the words above, is printed in Mrs. Davis's *Jefferson Davis*, II. 790. Mrs. Davis relates how Stanton's consent was secured, through John W. Garrett.

[2] Representative from Ohio 1849–1858, 1871–1873, minister to Mexico 1866–1868.

[3] *I. e.*, at the beginning of December, 1866.

˙ To meet this objection of Genl. Grant, on the 25th. of Oct. 1866, the President prepared a letter to the Secretary of War, (Mr. Stanton,) in these terms: "You will please instruct Genl. Ulysses S. Grant, commanding the armies of the U. S., to proceed to Mexico or its vicinity, there to act in concert with and as an adviser of L. D. Campbell, Esq." etc. This letter, however, was submitted to the Cabinet on the day next succeeding its date, when, after full consideration, it was decided, as the opinion of the Heads of Depts., that as the duty asked of Genl. Grant was of a civil character, and might, if questioned, give rise to doubts as to the authority of the Government to send him on such a mission, the communication for the Sec. of War was modified so as to state the object of the embassy and " to ask that you will request Genl. Grant to proceed to some point on our Mexican frontier most suitable and convenient for communication with our Minister, or (if Genl. Grant deems it best) to accompany him to his destination in Mexico, and to give him the aid of his advice in carrying out the instructions of the Sec. of State," etc.

The above quoted letter was dated the 26th Oct. 1866, and was sent to the War Dept. the succeeding day. In the afternoon of the same day the Sec. of War enclosed the reply of Genl. Grant, as follows:

" The same request was made of me one week ago today, verbally, to which I returned a written reply, a copy of which is herewith enclosed. On the 23d instant the same request was renewed in Cabinet meeting, where I was invited to be present, when I again declined, respectfully as I could, the mission tendered to me, with reasons. I now again beg most respectfully to decline the proposed mission, for the following additional reasons to wit: Now, whilst the army is being reorganized and troops distributed as fast as organized, my duties require me to keep within telegraphic communication of all the department commanders and of this city, from which orders must emanate.* Almost the entire frontier between the U. S. and Mexico is embraced in the depts. commanded by Genls. Sheridan and Hancock, the command of the latter being embraced in the military division under Lieut. Genl. Sherman—three officers in whom the entire country has unbounded confidence. Either of these general officers can be instructed to accompany the American Minister to the Mexican boundary, or the one can through whose command the Minister may propose to pass in reaching his destination. If it is desirable that our Minister should communicate with me, he can do so through the officer who may accompany him, with but very little delay beyond what would be experienced if I were to accompany him myself. I might add that I would not dare counsel the Minister in any matter beyond the stationing of troops on U. S. soil, without the concurrence of the Administration. That concurrence could be more speedily had with me here than if I were upon the frontier. The stationing of troops would be as fully within the control of the commanding officer as it would of mine.

" I sincerely hope I may be excused from undertaking a duty so foreign to my office and tastes as that contemplated."

The President expressed some surprise at this result. He said that when on Wednesday, Oct. 17, 1866, he sent for Genl. Grant and mentioned the subject to him, he thought the General evinced satisfaction, if not pleasure at the proposed arrangement. Immediately after the

* It was not until March 2, 1867, that Army Hd: Qrs. were, by law, fixed at Washington.—May not the above correspondence have suggested Sec. 2 of the Act of that date? (*Note in the original.*)

interview, the President visited the State Dept. and informed the Secretary of the result. The next morning, according to appointment, Genl. Grant called at the Executive Mansion, and Col. Moore[4] was dispatched to the State Dept. to notify Mr. Seward that the General would either await him at the President's, or call on the Secretary at any hour he might designate. The Secretary requested Col. Moore to say to the President and Genl. Grant that the instructions had just been completed, and that he would at once bring them to the President. (The State Dept. at that time occupied the locality now covered by the north wing of the Treasury Building.)[5] The Secretary accordingly made his appearance, and the instructions prepared for Mr. Campbell were read to Genl. Grant, to ascertain whether or not he had any suggestions to make. He said he had none to submit. On the succeeding Sunday Genl. Grant addressed a letter to the President, dated Oct. 21, 1866, stating:

"On further and full reflection upon the subject of my accepting the mission proposed by you in our interview of Wednesday, and again yesterday, I have most respectfully to beg to be excused from the duty proposed. It is a diplomatic service for which I am not fitted, either by education or taste. It has necessarily to be conducted under the State Dept., with which my duties do not connect me. Again, then, I most urgently, but respectfully repeat my request to be excused from the performance of a duty entirely out of my sphere, and one too which can be so much better performed by others."

It was subsequently to the transmission of the above letter to the President that Genl. Grant declined to receive from Mr. Campbell the instructions of the Secretary of State.

For all the official communications upon this subject, see the package of papers, marked "Genl. Grant and Mexico."[6]

Reasons other than those stated by Genl. Grant were by some assumed to have influenced his action in the matter of the mission to Mexico, and prominent among them was supposed jealousy of Sherman. Just about this time the papers had published a rumor that Mr. Stanton would resign and be sent as Ambassador to Spain, and that he would be succeeded in the War Dept. by Genl. Sherman, who in Febry. 1866 had addressed a letter to the President, strongly endorsing his policy of reconstruction. The fact that such a letter had been written by him to the Presidt. had but recently become known, and but a short time had intervened since Mr. Johnson had read the communication to Genl. Grant, at its conclusion remarking that he thought of publishing it—a suggestion which the President said the General did not appear to relish.[7] It was therefore concluded by some that Genl. Grant was afraid that should he leave the country, Sherman would first be exalted

[4] The writer of these notes, private secretary to the President.

[5] From 1820 to October, 1866, the Department of State was located on the site now covered by the north part of the Treasury. In October, 1866, it leased the premises of the Washington Orphan Asylum, on Fourteenth Street near S Street, where it remained until 1875. The phrase shows that this portion of Colonel Moore's notes was not put into its present shape until the site had been "covered by the north wing of the Treasury Building"; the foundations of that wing were laid in April, 1867, and the construction was completed in 1869.

[6] See Welles's *Diary*, II. 621. As to the packages or bundles to which the diarist refers, and which are mostly now in the Library of Congress, see Professor Sioussat's introduction, *ad fin.*

[7] *Ibid.*, p. 607; *Sherman Letters* (ed. Thorndike, New York, 1894), p. 279.

to his own position as the head of the Army, and thence transferred to the office of Secy of War, and thus become his (Grant's) superior in office.

Oct. 26, 1866, Lieut. Genl. Sherman called upon the Presidt. After the positive declination or refusal of Genl. Grant to go to Mexico, the President sent for Genl. Sherman, and found that he was entirely willing to undertake the duty.[8] The Presidt. asked him when he would be ready to go,—"At once" was the prompt and soldierlike response.—A letter was on the 30th Oct. sent to the Sec. of War, saying that "Genl. Ulysses S. Grant having found it inconvenient to assume the duties specified in my letter of the 26th. instant, you will please relieve him from the same, and assign them in all respects to Wm. T. Sherman, Lieut. Genl. of the Army of the U. S." (see the papers marked "Genl. Grant and Mexico.")

Grade of General.—July 1866.

The President hesitated some time before he signed the bill "to revive the grade of General in the United States Army," which he approved July 25, 1866. He considered the law inexpedient and unnecessary, saying that Washington had never been tendered a higher compliment than the rank of Lieut. Genl., already possessed by Grant; that the war had entirely ceased, the army been largely reduced, and that an additional grade could not give more effect to Grant's services than had already been done by conferring upon him the rank he now enjoyed. Secy Stanton had also suggested that the bill should be materially [maturely?] considered prior to approval, as it partook of the nature of giving a title or a distinction, etc. He, however, finally recommended that the President should attach to it his signature.

While the bill was in the hands of the President, he told me that General Grant called at the Executive Mansion, and requested that when his name should be sent to the Senate for Genl., Sherman's should accompany it for Lieut. General. He thus took it for granted that he would undoubtedly receive the promotion, although the law expressly empowered the President to make the selection "from among those officers in the military service of the U. S. most distinguished for courage, skill, and ability, who, being commissioned as Genl., may be authorized, under the direction and during the pleasure of the President, to command the Armies of the U. States."

New Orleans Riot—July, 1866.

The President believed that the riot which occurred in the City of New Orleans, July 30, 1866, would have been averted if an answer had been sent to Genl. Baird's telegram of the 28th. asking the Secretary of War for instructions. This despatch was not seen by the President until some time after the riot, when at his suggestion all the papers on the subject in possession of the War Dept. were prepared for publication and sent to the Executive Mansion. In examining the correspondence the President for the first time saw Genl. Baird's despatch:—(See Secretary Stanton's and Col. Moore's testimony before the Congressional Committee on the New Orleans riots, contained in printed volume.)[9]

[8] *Sherman Letters*, pp. 280–283.

[9] *House Report No. 16*, 39 Cong., 2 sess., pp. 534–536, 546–547. General Absalom Baird was in temporary command at New Orleans in the absence of Sheridan, the general commanding the district. Baird's telegram may be seen in *Trial of President Johnson*, I. 152, or in Gorham's *Stanton*, II. 316; Stanton's explanation, *ibid.*, pp. 324–325.

Maryland Troubles—Oct. and Nov. 1866.[10]

The package of papers marked " Maryland and the District of Columbia " shows the anxiety and determination of the President to preserve peace in Baltimore when serious disorders were threatened just prior to the Nov. election. Genl. Grant was opposed to the interference of the military, his position being explained by his letter to the President dated Oct. 24, 1866, which concludes as follows: " It is a contingency I hope never to see arise in this country whilst I occupy the position of General-in-Chief of the Army, to have to send troops into a State *in full relations with the* Genl. Government, on the eve of an election, to preserve the peace. If insurrection does come, the law provides the method of calling out forces to suppress it. No such condition seems to exist now."

After some correspondence between the President, the War Dept. and Army Hd. Qrs., the President on the 1st of November 1866, requested the Sec. of War to take all measures necessary to ensure the safety of the seat of government, and on the next day addressed another communication to that officer, desiring that the attention of Genl. Grant should be called to the state of affairs in Baltimore, in order that measures of preparation and precaution might be adopted.

Gov. Swann[11] was much in consultation with the President in reference to the threatened troubles in Baltimore, urging that a knowledge of the fact that the Government was prepared to suppress disorder would prevent any serious riot.

Recruits embarked at New York for Texas were ordered to stop en route at Fort McHenry, there to remain until all apprehensions of difficulty had passed away.

Tennessee Troubles—July, 1867.

The following telegram of Genl. Grant was deemed in striking contrast with his views in reference to Federal interference for the preservation of peace in Maryland:

" LONG BRANCH, N. J.
" July 23, 1867.

" To the
Hon: E. M. Stanton,
Secretary of War.

" Genl. Dent, with despatches from Genl. Thomas,[12] arrived before your telegram. I directed Genl. Thomas to give orders for the most vigorous use of the military to preserve order on election day, and not to wait until people are killed and the mob beyond control before interfering. I will direct Genl. Thomas to go directly to Memphis in person, but do not think there is any need of my going to Nashville."

U. S. GRANT,
General."

Tennessee had been by act of Congress, approved July 24, 1866, restored to her relations to the Union, and occupied precisely the same position to the Govt. as Maryland, when Genl. Grant declared his abhorrence to sending " troops into a State in full relations with the Genl. Government, on the eve of an election, to preserve the peace."

[10] The events can be followed in Mr. Knott's account in Nelson's *Baltimore,* pp. 558–562.

[11] Thomas Swann, governor of Maryland 1865–1869.

[12] Lorenzo Thomas, adjutant-general.

July 25, 1867.

When the President read me the despatch of Genl. Grant to Mr. Stanton, I at once inquired if the first-named had given any instructions upon the subject. He said none whatever, but that on the preceding Cabinet day (Tuesday, July 23d) the subject of the Tennessee troubles had been mentioned, when the Secretary (Mr. Stanton) proposed to use the military for the preservation of order. "This" (said the President) "was the very thing I desired, but I said nothing, and could scarce keep from smiling at the readiness with which the Secretary proposed to do in Tennessee what he and Grant earnestly opposed doing under similar circumstances in Maryland".[13]

January 4, 1867. { Dis. of Col. { Suffrage bill

The President had read to the Cabinet to-day his message returning to Congress, with his objections, the District of Columbia suffrage bill. All approved it, but Secry Stanton, who suggested that negro suffrage had to be tried, and that the experiment might as well begin in the District as any where else.[14]

"North Carolina"
Plan of Reconstruction.

January 30, 1867.—Gov. Orr, of S. C., Gov. Marvin, of Florida, Gov. Parsons, of Ala., Messrs. Haines and Boyden, of N. C.[15] had a protracted consultation this afternoon, with the President, as to a proposition to amend the Constitution which should be submitted to Congress as the Southern plan of reconstruction. It was proposed that North Carolina should take the initiative by the adoption of a proposition first to amend her own Constitution, and then that of the United States. The draft of the proposed amendments was in the handwriting of Mr. Lewis C. Haines, and after some discussion it was modified in several particulars upon the suggestion of the President.

January 31, 1867.—The above-named subject was again considered, the same persons being present, except Gov. Marvin. The President suggested the omission from the plan of the request that an assurance should be given the State that upon the adoption of the proposed amendment to the Constitution, Representatives and Senators should be admitted to Congress, and, further, that it should be simply a proposition to amend the Constitution of the State and to submit to the several States an amendment to the Federal Constitution, similar in very many of its provisions to that proposed by the 39th. Congress. The President sent me in the evening to call on Messrs. Orr, Haines, and Boyden at the Ebbitt House, with the suggestion that the proposition should contain, *first,* the amendment to the Federal Constitution, and *next* the suggestions in reference to the Constitution of the State.

In the discussion upon these propositions, it seemed to be the opinion that if they should be sustained by all the Southern States and presented with the influence of a united front, they would operate as a

[13] See Welles, III. 140-141.

[14] The discussion is reported by Welles, III. 3-6.

[15] James L. Orr, governor of South Carolina 1865-1868; William Marvin, provisional governor of Florida in 1865; Lewis E. Parsons, provisional governor of Alabama in 1865; Lewis Hanes, elected to Congress in 1866 but not seated, and in 1867 agent of North Carolina in Washington; Nathaniel Boyden, representative from North Carolina 1868-1869.

flank movement against and defeat the Radical programme, which, as was then supposed, it had already been demonstrated could not be adopted by a vote of the States. Govr. Orr told Colo. Moore in the evening that he had been informed by Representative Bingham, of Ohio, that the article for the exclusion of certain persons from office, embraced in the constitutional amendment proposed by Congress, was the work of Thad. Stevens; that it had been defeated in a full committee, but in the absence of Fessenden and Washburne, of Illinois, on account of sickness, Stevens had succeeded in obtaining a reconsideration of the vote, and the adoption of the article as a part of the plan. (See the papers marked " Reconstruction-Proposition to amend the Federal Constitution and the Constitution of North Carolina.")

February 9, 1867.

The President visited Mr. George Peabody this morning, at Willard's Hotel, as a mark of respect to one who had made such liberal provision for the cause of education in the South.[16]

February 14, 1867.

The President is evidently deeply impressed with the necessity of some effort to prevent the extreme measures proposed by the majority in Congress. Mr. Banks, of Mass.[17] visited him this morning. Before being admitted to the President's office, Mr. Banks said to me that in his view there should be some one in the Cabinet who could be approached by those who were in opposition to the President, and who could thus became a channel of communication between the Executive and Congress. He suggested Horace Greeley as Postmaster General, in place of Mr. Randall,[18] and his great anxiety in reference to reconstruction seemed to be lest, by admitting representatives from the " Rebel States," the disloyal element might again preponderate in those States, and perhaps in Congress. He gave the South credit for having men of great ability, who would be able to exercise much influence in the legislative councils of the nation.

At lunch I mentioned the subject to the President. He said it would not take him long to send for Mr. Greeley and that he could not perceive that any member of his Cabinet gave him any strength with the country. He (the President) believed that by appointing Grant as Sec. of War, Farragut as Sec. of the Navy, Chas. F. Adams as Sec. of State, and Greeley as Postmaster General, he could settle the question in two hours. He said, however, that such a course would occasion harsh feelings on the part of some of the Cabinet officers who would thus be relieved, and to some of whom he was much attached. I asked him if there was no way in which he could carry out such plans? He replied that he did not know that there was; and as the subject was evidently painful to him, I let the matter drop.

March 2, 1867.

The veto of the military reconstruction bill[19] was approved by all the members of the Cabinet, except Mr. Stanton.

[16] The Peabody Fund had been established in the preceding year.
[17] Nathaniel P. Banks.
[18] Alexander W. Randall of Wisconsin.
[19] Richardson, *Messages of the Presidents*, VI. 498–511.

March 4, 1867 { Military appro-
             { priation bill.

The President and Cabinet went to the Capitol this morning, to be present at the adjournment. The President took with him, unsigned, the military appropriation bill, the second section of which requires that all military orders from the President and Sec. of War shall pass through Genl. Grant. President Johnson had determined that he would not approve a bill containing such an objectionable feature. Each member of the Cabinet, however, was asked his opinion upon the subject, and it was concluded (at the Capitol) that the President should approve the bill, under protest, which was done. When the President asked the Secretary of War if he was in favor of a protest, the reply was "I make no objection to it." "But", said the President, "I wish to know whether you approve of a protest?" the secretary: "I approve your taking whatever course you may think best."

May 2d, 1867. { Purchase of
              { Russian America.

The President expressed the belief today that had it not been for the War Dept. all of our troubles would long since have been healed. He said he was convinced that that Dept. had thrown every obstacle in the way of the consummation of his plans for restoration. In this connection he alluded to the course of Secretary Stanton on the Russian-American treaty, remarking that when the question first came before the Cabinet he (the President) had merely listened to the discussion, without taking part *pro* or *con,* and that, so far as he could judge, it was determined unanimously that the acquisition was a desirable one. Mr. Stanton sustained the treaty in Cabinet, and thought it ought to be consummated. Subsequently, in a conversation with the Sec. of War, the President alluded to the evident gratification of Mr. Seward upon the ratification of the treaty. "Yes", said Mr. Stanton, with a significant look, "you don't know the half of it," and then proceeded to criticize the acquisition, declaring that it was a country of ice and rock; that $7,000.000 in gold were equal to $10,000,000 in currency, the yearly interest upon which was $600,000; that a territorial government, with the necessary military force, would create an annual expenditure of more than a million; and that during war it were better that it should be in the hands of a friendly Power than in our possession, as we must take means for its defence. The President told me he was surprised at the Secretary's remarks, and had concluded that because it had added to Mr. Seward's popularity before the country, Mr. Stanton was somewhat envious, and now wished to depreciate the value of Alaska as an acquisition. The President seemed inclined to believe that Mr. Stanton had originally favored the treaty because he believed that it would eventually become unpopular and bring odium upon Mr. Seward, when Mr. Stanton would feel himself at liberty to denounce the purchase and decry its wisdom.

In the latter days of April, 1867, the music stand was erected in the President's grounds for the summer. When the workmen were raising the flag-pole, the President remarked that he was present when the stars and stripes were first raised in the grounds by Presidt. Lincoln; that as Mr. Lincoln hoisted the colors, they somehow or other became entangled, and split; that although he (Mr. Johnson) was not superstitious, the incident at the time made an impression on his mind that it had been difficult entirely to efface.

Friday, Apl. 5, 1867.

Cabinet met at nine o'clock this morning, in accordance with a request of Atty. General Stanbery made the evening before.—The object of the meeting was to decide what should be done upon the application made to the Supreme Court of the U. S. by Gov. Sharkey and R. J. Walker for an injunction to restrain the President from executing the military reconstruction act. It was agreed by the Cabinet that the Attorney Genl. should appear before the Court at 12 o'clock to-day and resist the motion—the only Secretary not expressing an opinion being Mr. Stanton, who said he was willing to defer in the matter to the judgment of the Attorney General.[20]

The President considered this another attempt at evasion, and reiterated the belief that if it had not been for the pernicious influence exerted by the War Dept. over the " extreme gang " in Congress, during the first session of the 39th Congress, all the troubles that now divided the people would long since have been brought to a close. A gentleman had informed him that before Mr. Stanton became Secy. of War he heard Mr. S. allude to President Lincoln as " a damned baboon, grinning over the misfortunes of the country."

April, 1867.

A Mrs. Hodges, whose husband is a clerk of the House Judiciary Committee engaged in the impeachment investigation, called upon and informed the President that it was a " regular understanding " that if the Committee could not obtain sufficient testimony to impeach the President, they were to manufacture it, and, for the purpose of gold speculations, would bring in a resolution of impeachment at the Session to meet on the first Wednesday in July. (See her " developments " in the package marked " Dunham, alias Conover.")[21]

August 1, 1867.— { Mr. Stanton
{ reqnested to resign, etc.

The President directed me to-day to write a letter in the following terms, viz:

" *Sir:* Public considerations of a high character constrain me to say that your resignation as Secretary of War will be accepted. Very respectfully yours,

ANDREW JOHNSON.

" To the Honorable Edwin M. Stanton," etc.

The President said that for a year past Mr. Stanton must have seen that his resignation would at any time have been acceptable to the Executive. When the above letter was written Genl. Grant had just had an interview with the President, having been sent for. The President informed him of his intentions with regard to Mr. Stanton, and that he would be pleased to have the General act as Secretary of War. Genl. Grant urged that such a step would be impolitic, and that those who sought Mr. Stanton's removal were generally persons who had opposed the war. Besides, there were many claims pending in the War Dept. of which he (Grant) knew nothing, and of his ability to determine which he entertained serious doubts. The President replied that it could

[20] Mississippi *v.* Johnson, 4 Wallace 492. William L. Sharkey was governor of Mississippi ; Robert J. Walker had been senator from that state 1836–1845, and then (1845–1849) Secretary of the Treasury.

[21] The wife of Charles A. Dunham, *alias* Sanford Conover, had had a similar tale of subornation of perjury against Johnson in respect to the assassination of Lincoln. See Welles, III. 143–146.

not be said that he (Mr. Johnson) had opposed the war; that his action was not based upon any personal hostility toward Mr. Stanton, but upon public considerations of a high character; that as to pending claims, they could be examined and settled by a special commission or referred to Congress; and that it was not his wish to place the general in the attitude of seeking the place now tendered him.

Genl. Grant replied that he would not shrink from the performance of any public duty that might be imposed upon him; but reiterated his opinion as to the impolicy of the proposed removal.[22]

Aug. 5, 1867.

Was instructed by the President to deliver to Mr. Stanton, in person, the letter asking him to resign, the date having been changed to Aug. 5. Called at his room in the War Dept. twice, (not having found him in the first time,) and at about 10.15 A.M. delivered to him the letter. Found him in company with a gentleman, and I therefore merely handed him the letter, and retired.

Aug. 5, 1867. Mrs. Surratt.

The President, having heard that there was a recommendation in favor of Mrs. Surratt, sent today for the papers upon which was endorsed his approval of the finding and sentence of the Military Commission for the trial of the assassination conspirators. Forwarded with the papers was a recommendation of the Court for a commutation of the sentence in the case of Mrs. Surratt from hanging to imprisonment for life. The President very emphatically declared that he had never before seen the recommendation. He was positive that it had never before been brought to his knowledge or notice, and explained to me the circumstances attending the signing of the order to carry into effect the sentence of the commission. He distinctly remembered the great reluctance with which he approved the death warrant of a woman of Mrs. Surratt's age, and that he asked Judge Advocate Genl. Holt, who originally brought to him the papers, many questions, but that nothing whatever was said to him respecting the recommendation of the Commission for clemency in her case. He had been sick, but when he signed the papers his mind was as clear as it had ever been. Besides, the recommendation did not appear in the published proceedings of the trial, by Benn Pitman, prepared and issued by authority of the Secretary of War,[23] and he felt satisfied that it had been designedly withheld from his (the President's) knowledge.

August 6, 1867—Mr. Stanton.

At about 11.45 A.M. Mr. Stanton's reply was received. It was dated the 5th, and will be found in the papers marked " Hon. E. M. Stanton ".[24] The President did not evince much, if any surprise, and thought that Mr. Stanton had pursued a course which neither he nor his friends could sustain before the country. He said he would leave Mr. Stanton hanging on the sharp hooks of uncertainty for a few days, and then suspend him from office.

[22] Grant then added a letter, of the same date, the text of which may be seen in Gorham's *Stanton*, II. 394–395.

[23] *The Assassination of President Lincoln and the Trial of the Conspirators*, compiled and arranged by Benn Pitman, recorder of the commission (Cincinnati and New York, 1865). The manner in which the record was presented to the President and in which his signature to the executive order was obtained is discussed in Dewitt's *Assassination of Abraham Lincoln*, pp. 133–137, 283–287; but see also Rhodes, V. 157.

[24] *Trial*, I. 149; Richardson, *Messages*, VI. 584; Gorham, II. 395–396.

Aug. 9, 1867.

The President seems much relieved by the course he has taken in
the case of Mr. Stanton, and is satisfied that public opinion will not
sanction the position assumed by the Secretary.

Aug. 11, (Sunday), 1867.

The President and Genl. Grant had an interview. The President told
the Genl. of his intention to make a change in the War Dept. by suspending Mr. Stanton, remarking that the place thus made vacant must
be filled, and the question was, whether it would not be better that the
Genl. should be made acting Secretary than that a stranger should be
selected for the position. As the Commanding Genl. of the army, he
understood the wants and interests of the service, and besides was in-
timately connected, by the reconstruction acts, with their execution.
The President wished to know if Genl. Grant would take the place, if
appointed. Genl. Grant replied that he would of course obey orders.
The President then said that he thought he had the right to ask if there
was any thing between them, (the Genl. and himself). He had heard
it intimated that there was, and he would now really like to know how it
was. Genl. Grant replied that he knew of nothing personal between
them, and then alluded to the difference of opinion between the President and himself respecting the constitutional amendment and the reconstruction acts.[25] The interview here ended, and the President then
directed me to bring to him the letter which had already been prepared
suspending Mr. Stanton. The President said he was strongly inclined
not merely to say "you are hereby *suspended* from office as Secry. of
War," but "you are hereby suspended and *removed* from office as Secry
of War."

Before the question was determined, however, Mr. Seward called,
and the President accompanied him to church. The President also directed me today to write a communication appointing Genl. Grant Sec.
of War ad interim.

Aug. 12, 1867. (Monday.)

Col. Moore, by order of the President, delivered to Mr. Stanton the
letter suspending him from office. The Secretary read it, and said,
"I will send an answer."

Col. M. then proceeded to Army Head Qrs. and delivered to Genl.
Grant the letter appointing him Sec. of War ad interim. He deliberately
read it, folded it up, and said "Very well."

About half-past 12 p.m. Genl. Schriver handed to the President Mr.
Stanton's reply to the letter suspending him from office.[26]

When the President read the letter to me, he said "the turning
point has at last come; the Rubicon is crossed," adding, "You do not
know what Mr. Stanton has said and done against me." He then referred to a report prepared at the War Dept. upon a resolution of the
House of Reps., in which was embraced a list of murders alleged to
have been committed by rebels in the South, not called for by the inquiry, and respecting which the Sec'ry had declared that when it was
laid before the House the President would be thrust from office without
a moment's delay.

[25] Welles, III. 167.
[26] *Trial.* I. 148, 149; Richardson, *Messages*, VI. 583-584.

August 13, 1867.

Speaking of Mr. Stanton and his letter denying the President's authority to suspend him, the President said that Mr. Stanton was one of the most earnest members of the Cabinet in denouncing the constitutionality of the tenure of office act. He was so decided in his expressions that the President, who then had also under consideration the supplemental reconstruction act, requested that Mr. Stanton, Mr. Seward, and Mr. Welles should prepare a veto, as he (Mr. Johnson) had his hands too full to give the subject the attention which it merited.[27] The veto was accordingly prepared, Mr. Seward writing it, Mr. Stanton furnishing the authorities, and Mr. Welles giving some references upon the question which the bill involved. The President and Secretary Welles said that on the occasion referred to, Mr. Stanton, in language as strong as that used by Senator Sherman when the measure was before the Senate, declared that no person of proper sense of honor would remain in the Cabinet when asked to resign. When Mr. Stanton had thus expressed himself, the President said he did his best to cause the Secretary to understand that his resignation would be agreeable. It seemed to be well understood that the bill had been passed for the purpose of retaining Mr. Stanton in President Johnson's Cabinet.

Aug. 14, 1867.

The President to day, in speaking of the Hon. Mr. Groesbeck, of Cincinnati, Ohio,[28] said he was thoroughly familiar with our currency system, and was eminently qualified for the Treasury portfolio.

Aug. 17, 1867.

The President issued an order to day for the removal of Genl. Sheridan as Commander of the 5th District, believing that he was acting in a most arbitrary manner. In sending it to Genl. Grant, he wrote him a sort of personal note, saying that "before you issue instructions to carry into effect the enclosed order, I would be pleased to hear any suggestions you may deem necessary respecting the assignment to which the order refers." The President, in writing the note, said to me that if there were any good reasons against his order, Genl. Grant could call upon him and state them; that he presumed the General would of course oppose the order, as in his letter of the 1st Aug., 1867, he had protested against the proposed removal of Stanton and Sheridan, intimating that the change would produce a revolution.[29] Contrary to the President's expectations, Grant sent a *written* communication, of this date, urgently asking that the order be not insisted on, and which will be found in the package marked "Major Genl. P. H. Sheridan and the 5th Military District."[30]

Aug. 19, 1867.

The President replied to Grant in a forcible letter of this date. The General came over to see the President, and, after a brief conversation, acquiesced in the President's reasons for the change of commanders in the Fifth Military District, expressing the belief that Sheridan, who he said was familiar with the Western country, would do admirably in a

[27] February 26, 1867. Welles, III. 50–51.

[28] William S. Groesbeck, who in the ensuing impeachment trial was counsel for the President.

[29] *House Ex. Doc. No. 57*, 40 Cong., 2 sess., p. 1.

[30] *Ibid.*, p. 4.

command in the Indian region. He added, however, that it had been rumored that first Sheridan would be removed by the President, then the other district commanders, and finally himself. The President smiled, and reminded the General that long ago he had desired him to act as Sec. of War. The General replied "yes, he did not see the use of a civilian as Sec. of War," and gave the President to understand that after all the removal or suspension of Mr. Stanton was not a bad thing.

In narrating the above, the President said that when the proposition to remove Sheridan was submitted to the Cabinet, Mr. Welles alone favored it—the other—especially Messrs. McCulloch and Browning—appearing absolutely frightened at the very idea.[31]

Aug. 24, 1867.

On the 22d Genl. Grant referred to the President a telegram of the previous day from Surgeon Hasson, saying that Genl. Thomas[32] was in West Virginia, suffering from a disordered liver, and expressing the belief that it would be dangerous for the General to proceed to New Orleans, (to relieve Sheridan,) where the yellow fever was very prevalent. The President thought that this was a favorable indication that Providence was aiding him—his desire, in the first instance, having been to send Hancock to relieve Sheridan, but Thomas having been finally selected, because he was know[n] to be a Radical in his views, and one to whom that party could offer no objection. At the same time, however, he thought that Hancock was the better man of the two for New Orleans—being a splendid looking soldier, of most courteous bearing, firm and decided, and withal of considerable ability. He had not, besides, been mixed up with political matters, and would go to New Orleans unprejudiced.

When, therefore, Grant sent over the Surgeon's certificate and recommended a suspension of the order, the President concluded that it should at once be changed. This he did not do, however, until today, (the 24th,) when he altered the order so as to send Hancock to New Orleans, and leave Thomas, on account of the "unfavorable condition" of his health, in command of the Dept. of the Cumberland.[33]

In speaking of the Cabinet meeting on the previous day, the President remarked that Grant had argued that it would not do to correct the District Commanders in what they did, as such interference must tend to lessen their influence in their commands. He had also actually argued that the commanders of military districts were heads of Depts., in the sense intended in the clause of the Constitution which declares that Congress "may by law vest the appointment of such inferior officers as they think proper in the President alone, in the courts of law, or in the heads of departments."[34]

Aug. 26, 1868.

The President issued today his modified order, retaining Thomas in command of the Dept. of the Cumberland, assigning Hancock to the 5th Military District, and ordering Sheridan to the Dept. of the Missouri. He also ordered that Canby relieve Sickles in the command of the Second Military District.

About three p.m. Aug. 27, the President received from Grant a letter, dated the 26th, protesting against the former's order in reference to the 5th Military District. The General urged—

[31] Welles, III. 149–155.
[32] Major-General George H. Thomas.
[33] *House Ex. Doc. No. 57,* 40 Cong., 2 sess., pp. 6–7.
[34] Welles, III. 182–183, 186–187.

1st. That as Thomas himself had not been heard from directly, there was no present necessity for modifying the order of the 17th, and that unless there were some grave public reasons, no officer should be sent to New Orleans at this time, (on acct. of the prevalence of yellow fever.)

2d. That if Sheridan were immediately withdrawn, there would remain in command no officer of the rank required by law, (Brigadier Genl.) He assumed, therefore, that the President would at least modify his order in this respect.

3d. That the laws devolved upon him (Grant) certain duties, and that he would not consent to yield any of the authority they vested in him, but on the contrary would insist upon its exercise. He admitted the right of the President to assign commanders to the districts, but thought that as he was, under the laws, responsible to a considerable extent for their execution, he should be consulted. He would, however, issue the order necessary to carry out the assignment directed by the President, but must object to the details.

4. That never mind whether the country should judge right or wrong, this act of the President would be interpreted as an effort to defeat the reconstruction measures of Congress. Such a movement, on the part of the President, would only tend to disquiet and financial difficulties, and must lead to the adoption of more stringent measures in regard to the South.

The Genl. concluded by saying that he had sent this communication to the President because he was greatly in earnest.

The President, after having read the above letter in my presence, handed it to me. I read it, and at the request of the President, expressed an opinion as to its contents. The President then pronounced it insubordinate in tone, and said that he hardly believed any answer could be necessary; that if it were even published naked and alone, it would, in the minds of all sensible persons, condemn the author; but that as it was late in the afternoon, he would not determine whether or not he would answer it; early in the morning, however, he would let me know his decision.

Aug. 28, 1867.

The President informed me this morning that he had determined to send for Genl. Grant, and discuss with him kindly, but firmly the positions assumed in the latter's letter. If the result of the interview should not be satisfactory, a written reply could then be prepared. Genl. Grant was accordingly sent for, and in a few moments made his appearance.

The interview did not last very long. To use the President's own words, "After a full and free conference upon the various points of objection raised in Genl. Grant's letter, the General himself proposed to withdraw the communication". The President assenting, the Genl. took the latter with him, and shortly afterwards sent a formal request for permission for its withdrawal, to which the President formally responded.

The President said that in the course of the conversation he told Genl. Grant that the letter could do him (the President) no harm; that he could reply to it as successfully as he had answered his previous communication; and that it would do the Genl. more harm than it would him, (the President). President Johnson reminded Genl. Grant that at the Cabinet meeting the day before he (Grant) had asked to be excused from attending Cabinet sessions, as he did not wish to participate in political discussions, and had requested that he might be sent for when military matters were to be considered; also that the President had replied that it was entirely a matter of option with the General whether he engaged in such discussions or not. It now seemed (said the President to Genl. Grant) that while the General was making these suggestions, this very letter, which amounted to a sort of political essay, was being copied for his signature at Army Headquarters. The President further suggested that if every order he gave was to provoke a political essay from the General, it would be impossible for the Executive and the head of the War Dept. to work together; that the General must know that there were persons whose interests it would be to create misunderstanding between them; and that he (the President) could not see the force of the General's arguments, especially those that referred to the authority conferred by law upon Grant, when the order itself expressly declared that the District Commanders were to exercise any and all powers conferred upon them by law—none other.

Genl. Grant then asked if he could withdraw the paper, saying that he would issue the order, as instructed by the President. It was accordingly published on the 29th, bearing date the 27th.[35] (See papers marked "Genl. Grant, Genl. Sheridan, and Secretary Stanton.")

Thursday, Nov. 21, 1867.

About 8-1/2 p.m. Col. Cooper[36] came into the Library at the Executive Mansion and told the President that John Morrissey had just been to see him, and had assured him that the House Judiciary Committee had resolved upon a proposition for impeachment, and that the result had been effected by a change of base on the part of Mr. Churchill, of N.Y., a member of the Committee.[37] The President was disposed to doubt the correctness of the information, but remarked that if it was correct, "so let it be." I at once went to make inquiry, and ascertained that Cooper's information was correct.

Friday, Nov. 30, 1867.

Read to the Cabinet the President's annual message, to which there appeared to be no objection.[38] Also, read to the Cabinet his inquiries growing out of the proposition to suspend him during the impeachment trial. The Cabinet unanimously determined that the power of suspension was one that could not be constitutionally exercised.

The President was much gratified, and remarked to me, after the adjournment of the Cabinet, that the day had produced great results. The time for mere defence had now passed, and he could stand on the offensive in behalf of the Constitution and the country.

Genl. Hancock's order, on assuming command of the 5th. Military District,[39] highly gratified the President, who characterized it as manly and statesmanlike.

December 12, 1867.

The Atty. Genl. (Mr. Stanbery) was quite anxious that the President

[35] Welles, III. 188–189. Grant's general order no. 81.

[36] Colonel Edmund Cooper, representative from Tennessee 1866–1867, assistant secretary of the Treasury 1867–1869, and an intimate friend of the President.

[37] John C. Churchill, representative 1867–1871. Welles, III. 238.

[38] Richardson, VI. 558–581.

[39] The celebrated order no. 40, dated November 29, 1867, emphasizing the supremacy of the civil power. See *The Civil Record of Major-General Winfield Scott Hancock during his Administration in Louisiana and Texas*, pp. 4–5, and F. E. Goodrich, *Life of Hancock*, pp. 245–246.

should at once communicate to the Senate the reasons for the suspension of Mr. Stanton, suggesting that under the tenure of office bill the 20 days began on the assembling of Congress on the 21st of Nov. Mr. Stanbery had prepared a very elaborate paper on the subject, while the President had expressed his views in a brief, dignified history of the case, covering but a few pages. This, the President believed, was all that the question required. Mr. Stanbery, however, thought the case presented an excellent opportunity for the President's vindication, and therefore urged that his paper should be sent to the Senate. To-day the President caused me to read the message prepared by the Attorney General to Messrs. Stanbery, Welles, and Browning, and they discussed at some length the questions it contained.[40]

December 15, 1867.

The President yet thinks his message in Mr. Stanton's case would perhaps have been the best that could have been sent in. He says, however, that several Senators and other persons had told him that the one he had sent to the Senate contained the only explanation they had seen of the New Orleans riot.

He said that he understood from reliable authority that General Grant had considerable feeling about Secy. Stanton's letter yielding to him the War office. It was understood (the President remarked) that before Genl. Grant accepted the ad interim appointment he and Mr. Stanton had a " full and free conference," in which the latter advised the former to take the position. The General, however, seemed to think that in saying "inasmuch as the Genl. commanding the armies of the U. S. has been appointed ad interim, and has notified me that he has accepted the appointment, I have no alternative but to submit to military force." Mr. Stanton conveyed an intimation that he (Grant) was to some extent responsible for the President's action.

In further referring to Genl. Grant, the President observed that at the time of the removal of Sheridan, Grant appeared to have fallen into the idea that a revolution would be the result of such a proceeding; and that when the question was submitted to the Cabinet, Secretary Welles was the only one who sustained the President. Even Atty. Genl. Stanbery opposed the order, saying to the President that Mr. Wilson, the chairman of the House Judiciary Committee,[41] had declared that such a step would lead to impeachment, inasmuch as it would clearly indicate the intention of the Executive to hinder the execution of the reconstruction laws. The President said that when the removal of Sheridan was proposed, Mr. Browning's face actually seemed to grow thin at the suggestion, and that Mr. Randall exhibited nervousness and recommended delay.

The President has prepared a message, suggesting to Congress a vote of thanks to Genl. Hancock for the order issued by him in assuming command of the 5th District, which takes ground for the prevalence of civil law. He has not yet, however, determined to send it to Congress.[42]

Jany. 7, 1868.

I prepared today, by the President's direction, a letter of removal in the case of Mr. Stanton, and also a brief message to the Senate

[40] Richardson, VI. 583–594. Orville H. Browning was Secretary of the Interior.

[41] James F. Wilson, representative from Iowa 1861–1869, one of the managers of the impeachment on behalf of the House, and senator 1883–1895.

[42] Sent to the Senate under date December 18, 1867.

informing that body of the termination of Mr. S.'s connection with the War Dept. by dismissal.[43] The President said he desired to have these papers ready for signature at any moment, as he saw that the Senate were about to take up and act upon the suspension of the Secretary. I referred to the assertion made by some of the journals that Genl. Grant had expressed an intention to transfer the War Office to Mr. Stanton, in case the Senate should decide in the latter's favor. The President answered that Genl. Grant had told him that his action would be limited to withdrawing from the Department and leaving it in the hands of the President as fully as when it was conferred upon him, (the Genl.) The President expressed the opinion that perhaps it would be well for the Senate to reinstate the Secretary, as he could at once be removed, and in the mean time Genl. Grant be gotten rid of; indeed both would thus be disposed of, so far as the War Dept. was concerned. "Grant" (the President remarked) "had served the purpose for which he had been selected, and it was desirable that he should be superseded in the War Office by another."

January 14, 1868.

The President received last evening official notice of the action of the Senate, taken that day, refusing to concur in the suspension of Secy. Stanton. This morning Genl. Comstock, one of Grant's aides, delivered to the President a letter from the General, stating that he had last evening received official notice of the action of the Senate in the case of the suspension of Mr. Stanton, and that under the second section of the tenure of office law, his (Grant's) functions ceased from the time of the receipt by him of the Senate's resolution.[44]

The President exhibited great indignation at what he termed "Grant's duplicity". He said that no later than the preceding Saturday Grant had distinctly told him that if he found he could not, in his own opinion, properly resist the action of the Senate, he would at least leave the office of Sec. of War in the condition in which it was when he had been appointed to the position. This the President declared was not the first time that Genl. Grant had deceived him. In the case of the removal of Gov. Jenkins, of Georgia, by Genl. Meade, noticed in this morning's papers, Grant (the President said) had entirely deceived him, having given him to understand that no such removal would be made.

Genl. Grant attended Cabinet meeting to-day, (the 14th) and the President, in the presence of the Secretaries, referred to the War Dept. matter, asking the General if he did not distinctly tell the President that should the Senate reinstate the Secretary of War, and he (Grant) should not feel himself at liberty to resist such action, he would at least leave the office at the disposal of the President. This, the Presidt. said, the General acknowledged before the entire Cabinet, with an abashed look never to be forgotten.[45] Besides (continued the President) Genl. Grant attended the levee last evening, with his wife. Before coming he had received notice of the action of the Senate, and could then have notified me of what he intended to do, and at least have left me the option of making another selection in his place, if I deemed it proper to do so. He then alluded to an assertion that had beeen made that previous to Genl. Grant's attendance at the levee, the Genl. and Secretary Stanton had had a conference at the former's residence and agreed upon a

[43] The letter (*Trial*, I. 156) was not actually sent until February 21, 1868.

[44] McPherson, *Reconstruction*, p. 283.

[45] Welles, III. 259–262.

course of action, and laughed at the fact that the Radicals had actually legislated Grant, their favorite for the Presidency, out of the War Dept.

January 15, 1868.

Genl. Grant, in company with Gen. Sherman, called early this morning. After the interview closed, the President said to me that Genl. Grant had alluded to an article published in the Intelligencer of this morning, and headed " The Stanton affair," and remarked that it contained some things which he (Grant) did not understand to be true. The President replied that he had not yet read the article; and shortly after Grant and Sherman withdrew.

At the President's request, I read to him the article. and he said it was substantially true. Subsequently Secretary Welles came in, and when the subject was mentioned to him, said that he had read the article, and that it was a true statement of the case, so far as it related to what had taken place at the Cabinet meeting. The Secretary added that he was sorry some one had not been " present to take down the exact words, but more especially to paint Grant's confusion of face and manner;" that the General " acknowledged every thing the President said in regard to the understanding between them, and when the conversation was through, slunk away to the door in a manner most humiliating and pitiable."

January 16, 1868.

Secretary McCulloch, in describing the scene at the Cabinet meeting to Atty. Genl. Stanbery, (who was not present on the occasion,) conveyed the same idea as that expressed by Secretary Welles yesterday.

Jany. 17.—For proceedings of Cabinet on the Grant-Stanton matter see Vol. 4, scrap book, page 77.[46]

January 26, (Sunday) 1868—

The President said he intended to make a new military district, consisting of Maryland, Delaware, Virginia, and West Virginia, and to place Genl. Sherman in command, his headquarters to be in the War Dept., at Washington; that then it was his purpose to make Sherman Sec. of War ad interim.* He told me that yesterday evening week Genl. Sherman intimated to him that there was not the best of feeling between Mr. Stanton and Genl. Grant; that on the next morning (Sunday, the 19th.) Genl. Grant called at the Executive Mansion prior to going to Richmond. and in the course of conversation spoke of the insignificance to which Mr. Stanton could be reduced in his present position; that he (the President) referred to the law creating the office, and replied yes, that the Secretary would amount to nothing more than a clerk; that General Grant then said that he would not obey Mr. Stanton's orders, unless he knew they emanated from the President; that he (the President) replied that in pursuing such a course the General would do right; that he (the President) did not consider Mr. Stanton as authorized to act as Secretary of War; he had suspended him from office, and did not intend to recognize him.

The President then referred to a letter of Genl. Grant, delivered on the 24th by Genl. Comstock, viz: "I have the honor very respectfully

[46] Doubtless the scrapbook referred to by Welles, III. 262. It is at the Library of Congress.

* See package marked Genl. Sherman for his letters, declining to take a command at Washington. (*Note in original.*)

to request to have in writing the order which the President gave me verbally on Sunday, the 19th. instant, to disregard the orders of the Hon. E. M. Stanton as Secretary of War, until I know from the President himself that they were his orders."[47]

The President said to me that he did not think he would give the order; that the General had been very restive under Mr. Stanton, had evidently been very glad to get rid of him, had now put him back in the War Dept., and he thought he would let them fight it out. The President also alluded to a letter of Genl. Sherman, dated the 18th., in which that officer, in referring to Genl. Grant, says " he will call on you tomorrow, and offer to go to Mr. Stanton to say, for the good of the service and of the country, he ought to resign." (See papers marked " Genl. Sherman.")

January 28, 1868.—See, in the " Correspondence with Genl. Grant growing out of his vacation of the War Department," letter of Jany. 28, 1868, renewing his request of the 24th, and alluding to " gross misrepresentations " " purporting to come from the President," etc., etc.

In the same package of papers, will also be found the President's order upon the subject, dated Jan. 29, 1868, and Genl. Grant's reply dated the succeeding day.

January 29, 1868, the President dictated his reply to General Grant's letter of the 28th.

January 31.—Genl. Grant's letter of the 28 was today read to the Cabinet. The President then submitted his reply. It was declared to be correct, and met the approval of all the members of the Cabinet present, excepting Mr. Stanbery, who, not having attended the meeting of the 14th, could not of course say any thing with reference to the accuracy of the President's statements. The members present today, in addition to Mr. Stanbery, were Messrs. Seward, Welles, McCulloch, Randall, and Browning.[48]

February 3, 1868.—

The correspondence between the President and Genl. Grant was read today to Genl. Sherman. Genl. Sherman corroborated the statement made by Genl. Grant in his letter of the 28th, respecting the conversation which took place on Saturday, the 11th Jany, between the General, Lieut. General, and some members of Grant's staff, in which the latter expressed his views as to his duty under the tenure of office law, and said he would at once see the President upon the subject. Genl. Sherman told the President that Genl. Grant seemed to have made up his mind to await Mr. Stanton's written demand for the office, and then to have referred the subject to the President—thus, as the President held, conclusively showing that the General did contemplate holding on to the office for the President's instructions, and that for some cause or other he suddenly changed his intention. Genl. Sherman further said that Genl. Grant was very much angered at the course of Mr. Stanton, and seemed to have been thwarted in his plans by the action of the Secretary in taking such early possession of the War Office. General Sherman also said that General Grant had told him that Tuesday morning, when Mr. Stanton took possession of the War Dept., the Secretary had sent for him in the usual manner, by an orderly; that Genl. Grant was

[47] *Trial,* I. 240.
[48] Welles, III. 267, 268. The various letters alluded to are in McPherson, pp. 282–286.

indignant against him, declaring that he would never again enter the Dept. while Mr. Stanton was its head, unless sent for; and that Genl. Grant was deeply troubled by the condition which affairs had now assumed, and had become very obstinate in reference to the matter.[49]

February 4, 1868.

Genl. Grant's letter of the 3d, in reply to the President's communication of the 31st, was read to the Cabinet to-day.[50] It evoked expressions both of indignation and ridicule.

Attorney Genl. Stanbery said that aside from the facts in the case, the tone and taste of the letter struck him as most extraordinary.

Secretary Browning. It is the weakest and most disreputable letter that he could have written.

Secretary Welles. He has great ambition, and is a most remorseless man. That was shown in his campaign in Virginia.

Secretary McCulloch. His conversation here was exactly the contrary of what he asserts.

Mr. Secretary Browning. The letter is weak, false, and disreputable.

A suggestion was then made, which met with great unanimity, that an answer should be returned simply stating that the character of the communication was such as to preclude any further correspondence upon the subject. Atty General Stanbery thought that the acknowledgment of the letter should be made by the Private Secretary—not by the President, and in the course of the conversation Mr. Secretary McCulloch stated that General Grant seemed so greatly disturbed at the Cabinet meeting of the 14th. ultimo that it was not surprising that he did not recollect what he had then said.

Secretary Browning. How does he explain why he entered into an explanation as an excuse for not having called on Monday? If he had not promised, there was no necessity for any excuse.

The Attorney General then read the letter, reviewing it, as he proceeded, very severely.

February 5, 1868.

Mr. Stanbery called this morning, and the President caused to be read to him the reply he had prepared to Genl. Grant's letter of the 3d. The Attorney General earnestly urged that as the question was now one of veracity between the President and the General, the members of the Cabinet who were present at the Cabinet meeting of the 14th. ultimo should be called upon for a statement respecting the conversation which then took place. He reminded the President that he (Mr. S.) was an old lawyer, that he had been accustomed to watching cases, and he believed now was the moment to nail this whole affair by doing as he had suggested.[51]

February 6, 1868.

The President today issued an order creating the Military Division of the Atlantic, to be commanded by Lieut. Genl. Sherman, with his headquarters at Washington—the Genl. to assume command as early as may be practicable. The President thought this order would " set some persons to thinking."

[49] Sherman, *Memoirs* (1886), II. 425–428.

[50] Welles, III. 269–270.

[51] This course was taken. Welles, III. 271. The letters are in McPherson, pp. 289–291.

February 7, 1868.

The President, this morning, directed the withdrawal of the above-named order, and it was accordingly returned from Genl. Grant's Headquarters.

February 12th, 1868.

The President to-day renewed the order creating the Division of the Atlantic—omitting, however, the words, "You will direct Lieut. Genl. Sherman to assume command as early as may be practicable."

February 13, 1868.

The President today nominated Sherman "to be General by brevet in the Army of the U.S. for distinguished courage, skill, and ability displayed during the war of the rebellion".

February 15, 1868.

It is said that General Sherman objects to the nomination of General by brevet, as well as to the command of the new Military Division.[52] The President, in referring to the matter, said that when Sherman was in Washington, he conversed with him upon both of these subjects; that the General had expressed in writing his views in regard to the new command; but that when it was proposed to brevet him, he had objected in a way in which a diffident man would hesitate to accept such a distinction.

Monday, Febry. 17, 1868.

On Saturday, the 15th, it was suggested to John Potts, the Chief Clerk of the War Dept., that as in case of vacancy the law made him the custodian of all official papers in the Dept., he would be the proper person to be appointed Sec. of War ad interim, until Genl. McClellan or some other suitable person could be nominated to and confirmed by the Senate. The President's idea was to remove Mr. Stanton, appoint John Potts Secretary ad interim, and let him demand the papers, etc. of the War Dept. If Mr. Stanton refused to yield them, then the case was to be brought before the courts. Mr. Potts earnestly desired not to be placed in such a position, urging that he, as Chief Clerk, was the appointee of the Secretary; that if he should go to the Secretary and demand the papers, the Secretary could reply by his removal; that his relations with Mr. Stanton were of a very pleasant nature, and he did not wish to disturb them.

The President remarked this morning that if he could only find a proper person to act as Secretary ad interim, he would settle the War Department question without a moment's delay.

February 18, 1868.

The President entertains some idea of appointing Genl. Thomas, the Adjutant General, Secretary of War ad interim.

February 19, 1868.

The President received through Army Headquarters, this morning, Genl. Sherman's letter of the 14th. He was at a loss to know why the Genl. had not communicated directly with him, and although Sherman in most earnest terms asked to be relieved from the command of the New Military Dept., the President thought he would yet be pleased to come to Washington, remarking that he knew Mrs. S. wished to do so.

The President did not delay long in sending the following telegram:

52 See *The Sherman Letters*, pp. 300–310.

"To Lt. Genl. Wm. T. Sherman,
   "Saint Louis, Mo.
"I have just recd.,.with Genl. Grant's endorsement of reference, your letter to me of the 14th. instant. The order to which you refer was made in good faith, and with a view to the best interests of the country and the Service. As, however, your assignment to a new military division seems so objectionable, you will retain your present command.
                               "ANDREW JOHNSON."
A copy of the above was sent to Genl. Grant for his information.

                               ST. LOUIS, Feb. 19, 1868.
"*To the President:*
"Your very kind despatch is at hand. I cannot express under what deep obligations I am for your concession to my wishes.
                               WM. T. SHERMAN,
                               "Lieut. General."

                               Feb. 19—*continued.*
The President discussed the expediency of making Adjt. Genl. Lorenzo Thomas Sec. of War ad interim. He said he was determined to remove Mr. Stanton; that self-respect demanded it; and that if the people did not entertain sufficient respect for their Chief Magistrate to uphold him in such a measure, then he ought to resign.

                               Febry 20, 1868.
The War Dept. subject still under consideration in the mind of the President.
                               Febry 21, 1868.
The President entered the office promptly this morning, and immediately directed the preparation of the following-named papers:[53]
   1st.—The removal of Mr. Stanton and the apptmt. of Lorenzo Thomas, the Adjt. General, as Secretary of War ad interim.
   2d. A message notifying the Senate of the change.
   3d. A request to the Secretary of State to bring with him to Cabinet meeting the nomination of George B. McClellan as Minister to England.
   4th. A nomination for the apptmt. of George H. Thomas as a Lieutenant General by brevet, and a General by brevet.
   The President sent for Genl. Lorenzo Thomas, and handed him his letter of appointment, and also the removal of Mr. Stanton. He showed Genl. Thomas the laws upon the subject, remarking that he wished to proceed according to the Constitution and the laws, and advised the General to be accompanied by a witness when he delivered to Mr. Stanton the letter of removal. Genl. Thomas said he would take with him Genl. Williams, of the Adj. Genl's. Office,[54] and would report the result to the President.
   Before one o'clock P. M. Genl. Thomas returned, and reported that he had delivered to Mr. Stanton the President's communication, with the remark, "I am directed by the President to hand you this." Mr. Stanton (said Genl. Thomas) sat on the sofa, and after reading the paper, said, "Do you wish me to vacate at once, or am I to be permitted to stay long enough to remove my property?" "Certainly", I said; "act

[53] The first two are in *Trial,* I. 156.
[54] Major Robert Williams, brevet brigadier-general, assistant adjutant-general. The ensuing narrative agrees with Thomas's testimony, *Trial,* I. 418–419.

your pleasure ". I then showed him my order. He said " I wish you to give me a copy." I replied "Certainly, sir." I then returned to my office, a copy of the paper was made by Genl. Townsend,[55] and I certified it as Secretary of War ad interim. When I took it up to him, he said " I want some little time for reflection. I don't know whether I shall obey your orders or resist them."

The Senate was notified by message of the change made in the War Dept. and the nominations of Genl. McClellan and Genl. Thomas[56] were submitted, at the same time, to that honorable body.

February 22, 1868.

Genl. Thomas[57] was arrested at an early hour this morning. He went to the Executive Mansion in company with the Marshal, and then, at the President's suggestion, proceeded to the Atty General for advice. The President said the intention was to give bail and stand trial. Shortly after he sent for the Atty Genl., who came immediately.

Genl. Thomas was released on bail, and after calling at the office of the Atty. Genl., proceeded to the President's House and saw Mr. Johnson, relating to him the proceedings before Judge Cartter. He then went to the War Dept., and was summoned into the presence of Mr. Stanton, who, he said, was surrounded by several members of Congress. The Adjt. General gave the following account of the conversation that ensued: Mr. Stanton remarked that he understood that Genl. Thomas had been issuing orders as Secretary of War ad interim, and he ordered him to desist. Genl. Thomas replied that Mr. Stanton was no longer Secretary of War, but that he (Thomas) was, and would continue to issue orders as such. Mr. Stanton then ordered him to proceed to his own office as Adjt. General. Gen. Thomas positively refused to take any order from Mr. Stanton, and the order and refusal were repeated three times. Mr. Stanton replied " Very well "; then you may stand in the middle of the floor as long as you like. Upon the suggestion of Genl. Thomas, he and Mr. Stanton then went into an adjoining room, where Mr. S. repeated his orders, which the General declined to obey. Genl. Moorhead, a Representative from Pa.,[58] was present, and wrote the orders of the Secretary and the replies of General Thomas. In the course of the conversation, Genl. Thomas told Mr. Stanton that he had caused his (Thomas') arrest before breakfast, and that he had had nothing to eat or drink. Mr. Stanton replied that he thought Genl. Schriver[59] could supply a drink, and thereupon that gentleman produced a small bottle, containing a small drink, which Genl. Thomas took. Mr. Stanton then put his arm around Genl. T.'s neck, and run his fingers through his hair. He also sent to his house for a full bottle, which arriving, they drank together.

Mr. Stanbery and Mr. Welles came to see the President. After an earnest conversation, it was determined, upon the urgent recommendation of the Attorney General, to send to the Senate the name of Thomas Ewing, senior, of Ohio, for Secretary of War. Mr. Stanbery said he

[55] Colonel Edward D. Townsend, brevet major-general.

[56] George H.

[57] Lorenzo; arrested at Stanton's instance. See his testimony, *Trial*, I. 428–429.

[58] James K. Moorhead, representative 1859–1869. See his testimony in *Trial*, I. 170–174.

[59] Edmund Schriver, brevet major-general, in charge of the Inspection Bureau.

was not too old for the place;[60] that he was an able lawyer, an "old line Whig," and an earnest supporter of the President. The President had in the morning suggested Mr. Ewing's apptment. The nomination was prepared and taken to the Senate, but that body had adjourned after a very brief session.[61]

In the House of Reps. there was considerable excitement, and the Committee on Reconstruction presented a resolution of impeachment.

The President says that he has made an issue demanded by his self-respect, and that if he cannot be President in fact, he will not be President in name alone. I have (said he) taken a step which I believe to be right, and I intend to abide by it. I do not want to see this Government relapse into a despotism. I have ever battled for the rights and liberties of the People, and I am now endeavoring to defend them from arbitrary power.

February 23d, 1868 (Sunday.)

A message was prepared today in reply to the Senate resolution denying the power of the President to remove the Secretary of War and appoint a Secretary ad interim. It seems the message is at the instance of some of the Radical Senators, who it is said desire some reasons to justify them in opposing impeachment.

February 24, 1868—(Monday.)

The message above referred to, bearing date the 22d,[62] and the nomination of Mr. Ewing, were submitted to the Senate to-day. A large number of the City Police on duty at the Capitol—there seeming to be an apprehension of some demonstration against Congress. At the Executive Mansion affairs are very quiet.

Senator Doolittle[63] sent to the President this morning, in great haste, a note urging him to send a message to both Houses. The President said he would do nothing of the kind. The message he had prepared was in answer to a resolution of the Senate, and the House had therefore nothing to do with it.

The President, at about 6 P.M. today, received information of the vote on impeachment in the House of Reps.—126 to 47. He received the news very calmly, simply remarking that he thought many of those who had voted for impeachment felt more uneasy as to the position in which they had thus placed themselves than he did as to the situation in which they had put him.

February 25, 1868.

Matters very quiet at the Executive Mansion.

February 26, 1868.

Genl. Lorenzo Thomas was today released—Mr. Stanton declining to prosecute.

It is said that the Committee upon the subject are in "travail" over the articles of impeachment that are to be brought against the President —finding it difficult to agree.

February 28, 1868.

On Monday Genl. Emory,[64] commanding the Department of Wash-

[60] Gov. Thomas Ewing, formerly Secretary of the Treasury, Secretary of the Interior, and senator, was 78 years old at this time.

[61] See Col. Moore's testimony in *Trial*, I. 556–557.

[62] Printed in Richardson, VI. 622–627.

[63] James R. Doolittle of Wisconsin, senator 1857–1869.

[64] Maj.-Gen. William H. Emory.

ington, instructed the officer commanding the garrison of the city to send verbal orders to officers in charge of troops or posts *that all orders must come through proper channels.*

February 29, 1868.

The President, in very earnest terms, referred to the question of impeachment. He said: "They have impeached me for a violation of the Constitution and the laws. Have I not been struggling, ever since I occupied this chair, to uphold the Constitution which they are trampling under foot? I suppose I made Col. Cooper angry with me to-day. He wanted me to use the patronage of my office to prevent a judgment against me by the Senate! I will do nothing of the kind. If acquitted, I will not owe it to bribery. I would rather be convicted than buy acquittal."

Articles of impeachment were today reported from the Committee in the House of Reps.

March 7, 1868.

At seven o'clock P. M. today the Sergeant-at-Arms of the Senate presented to the President the summons to appear before the High Court of Impeachment.

March 8, 1868.

The President said that overtures had been made to Secretary Seward, to the effect that in the event of a change of administration he should be retained in office, provided he did nothing to interfere with the progress of impeachment. Mr. Seward's reply was, "I will see you damned first! The impeachment of the President is the impeachment of his Cabinet."

March 10, 1868.

Mr. Stanbery has determined to resign the office of Attorney General, that he may become one of the President's counsel in the impeachment trial—Unless he resigned, he said that the Radicals would charge that while he was the counsel of the President, he was in the pay of the United States. Besides he wished to devote his whole time and attention to the great work. Afterwards he might resume the office, provided the Senate would permit him to do so.

March 11, 1868.

Mr. Stanbery submitted today his resignation.

March 13, 1868.

The President declares that if his defence is not conducted according to his ideas, he will appear before the Senate in person and defend himself, saying that then, if he should be convicted, he alone could be blamed, if it followed as the result of plain speaking.

March 14, 1868.

The President and his counsel are in consultation. He is informed that since day before yesterday the troops have been under arms, furnished each with forty rounds of cartridges.

Received a rumor, at three o'clock, of the death of Hon. Thad. Stevens.[65] The President did not think it could be true, and compared Mr. Stevens to Vesuvius, which at times withdrew into itself all its heat and vapor, only to burst forth again in flames and lava. So he thought it must be with Mr. Stevens—a sort of temporary paralysis, which would be succeeded by a flow of living passion.

The rumor proved to be without foundation.

[65] Stevens did not die until August 11.

March 16, 1868.

Mr. Stanbery entered the Library this morning in excellent spirits. He said " I am now in regular training, like a prize-fighter. Every morning and evening, I have a man to come and rub me down, to keep in good condition. I feel that we will win, and that you, Mr. President, will come out all right. As the boys say, I feel it in my bones. Don't lose a moment's sleep, Mr. President, but be hopeful. When some things are done, we cannot tell if they be for good or for evil. I confess I felt a misgiving about this act of impeachment when it was first done; but now that it has been done, and the whole matter is to be considered, I see in it nothing but good. It gives you the great opportunity to vindicate yourself, as President, against every charge made against you. It gives you an opportunity to do so not only before the American people, but before the entire world—an opportunity such as you could never otherwise have had, to search and probe every thing connected with your official life—to show whether you are a traitor or not; to show whether or not your policy, when contrasted with theirs, is not the policy of wisdom; to show what would have been the result if it had been carried out, and to bring before the public the results of the course which your political opponents have pursued.

" Why, Mr. President, they call you a traitor to the party which elected you. I am one of that party. When I put the question to myself as to services, I find that I am far behind you in good works; for what did *I* do? All that I did was without loss or peril, while what *you* have done, has been in the face of all sorts of dangers and difficulties. From the first a Union man, do I feel that you have disappointed me in any hope I had in you? So far from it, if you had taken any other course, I should have been sadly disappointed and grieved. When you succeeded Mr. Lincoln, I said that the danger was that in his death the South had lost its best friend, and that you, stimulated by the injuries you had received from the Southern people, would not deal with them mercifully. That, Mr. President, was my fear, and entertaining this idea, I would not have entered your Administration at the time it was first formed. I came here the succeeding winter. I found you doing your best for reconciliation, and when you called me to Washington, I did not hesitate a moment. I have watched you day and night; I have been with you under all circumstances, and have been consulted by you upon every subject, from the beginning to the end of my connection with your Administration, and I have seen nothing which, had I been in your place, I would not have done myself.

" This impeachment trouble grows out of Mr. Stanton's removal. Let me recall a circumstance. When I came here I found Mr. Stanton in perfect harmony with you. While you were absent on your Western tour, Mr. Stanton and I rode to the Arsenal. We commenced talking about matters, and I said ' The President seems to confide more in you than in Seward.' ' Well ' he replied, ' I believe he does.' That was in August, 1866.

" Mr. President, if I can only keep well for this trial, I will be willing to be sick during the balance of my life. I know, sir, that you will come out of it brighter than you have ever shone."

The above is nearly a verbatim report of Mr. Stanbery's remarks, delivered with great earnestness, and considerable rapidity of utterance. He became so impressive and eloquent that, without his knowledge, I seized a pencil, and wrote in short-hand as he proceeded.

The President in referring to the remark made by Mr. Stanbery in respect to Mr. Stanton, said that it recalled to his mind the fact that about the time of the Western trip, Mr. Stanton cautioned him that Mr. Seward was a candidate for the Presidency.

Hon. Alex. H. Stephens, of Georgia, visited the President this morning. The President said that Mr. Stephens actually shed tears as he spoke of impeachment, and remarked " I have served with you in Congress ten years,[66] I have been with you in canvasses, I know you as well as you are known by any man, and now let me counsel you, as I would a brother, to make your own defence. No one can do it as well as yourself, and I believe your safety demands it."

March 17, 1868.

All the counsel are with the President this morning—Messrs. Stanbery, Curtis, Black, Evarts, and Nelson.[67] Mr. Curtis is reading the answer he has prepared to the articles of impeachment.

R. W. Latham[68] called to see the President, but as he was engaged with his counsel, Mr. L. sent for me. He said that last evening he had seen Senator Pomeroy,[69] who had authorized him to say to the President that as matters now stand conviction is a dead certainty, but that the resignation of the entire Cabinet will place him in a position, if he will act promptly—say not later than Thursday—to kill impeachment. Mr. Pomeroy suggests N. P. Banks for the Department of State, Robt. J. Walker for the Treasury—preferring, however, Smythe personally, but Walker, so far as the interests of the country are concerned; F. P. Stanton for the Navy Dept., and submits no names for the Interior and P. O. Depts., though he thinks the present Heads should be removed.[70] Mr. Latham told me that Pomeroy observed to him, " You may say to the President that I don't think he will do this, or take advantage of his position; that he relies more on his enemies than on his friends; that he will in all probability postpone action in these matters until his props are knocked from under him, and then he can do nothing. Did you ever see a blacksmith, who, having his iron heated, hesitated until it cooled? If so, what sort of a weld did it make? "

Mr. Latham continued: "F. P. Stanton and myself had a long talk with Stewart, of Nevada,[71] last night—a sort of caucus in this matter. He is the bitterest man in the Senate; but he said if this thing were done, it would destroy impeachment entirely. He went so far as to say that if he were in the President's place, he would put Butler in one of these offices rather than stand in his present position."

Mr Latham also said that Senator Pomeroy declared that impeachment was viewed as a *political*, not a *legal* question, and that he would

[66] 1843–1853.

[67] Henry Stanbery, Benjamin R. Curtis, Jeremiah S. Black, William M. Evarts, and Thomas A. R. Nelson. Later Black's place was taken by William S. Groesbeck.

[68] R. W. Latham of New York was at this time president of the Washington, Georgetown, and Alexandria Railroad, with offices in Washington. He appears to have had some political influence in Virginia.

[69] Samuel C. Pomeroy, senator from Kansas 1861–1873.

[70] Nathaniel P. Banks, representative from Massachusetts 1853–1857, 1865–1873, 1875–1877, 1889–1891; Robert J. Walker, of Mississippi, senator 1836–1845, secretary of the Treasury 1845–1849; H. A. Smythe, collector of the port of New York; Frederick P. Stanton of Virginia, representative from Tennessee 1845–1855.

[71] William M. Stewart, senator 1865–1875, 1887–1905.

be compelled to vote for it, unless the President should give him some excuse for a contrary course; that a million of dollars would not save the President as the case at present stood. Mr. L. declared that Pomeroy had said to him, " We are not satisfied with Stanton; we are not satisfied with our position in respect to him. We would be glad to have an excuse to get rid of him in some way, and there must be a general change in the Cabinet before that can be done. The country is not satisfied with Stanton's position, and the President is entitled to have his friends in the Cabinet." The Senator also told Mr. Latham that Secretary McCulloch had himself defeated the President's nominees—Col. Cooper for Asst. Secretary of the Treasury, and Genl. Wisewell[72] as Commr. of Internal Revenue.

Mr. Latham, in conclusion, desired me to remind the President that Banks, Walker, and Stanton were old Democrats, " just like the President," and that they were no more " rabid " than the President to-day.

When I mentioned the above conversation to the President " for what it was worth," he exhibited considerable indignation, remarking " I will have to insult some of these men yet."

During a visit to the Capitol to-day, Senator Reverdy Johnson[73] expressed anxiety that " the President should do something to help himself," and appeared to entertain the opinion that a change should be made in the State and Treasury Depts.

March 18, 1868.

Senator Pomeroy called this morning before ten o'clock, and had a long interview with the President. In referring to the Senator's visit, immediately after he had left the Executive Mansion, the President said that the conversation was of a general character; that the Senator said he had called to see if the President had any suggestions to make; that in reply he (the President) had observed that he had nothing particular to suggest, but would be really pleased to receive the views of Mr. Pomeroy. The Senator (the President said) talked very kindly, and made no recommendation in reference to the Cabinet. He, however, referred to Mr. Seward, remarking that at one time the Secretary was particularly obnoxious to the majority in Congress, but really seemed now to be less so; and that as to Mr. McCulloch, some of Mr. Chase's friends thought that the Secretary was opposed to the Chief Justice, but that the latter deemed Mr. McCulloch his friend. The President replied that in consequence of Mr. McCulloch's timidity, some of his acts had been misconstrued; that he believed the Secretary to be a friend of Mr. Chase; that even his (the President's) motives had been misunderstood; that as he had often declared, the measure of his ambition would be filled if he could perfect the work of reconciliation he had begun; that he was not seeking the Presidency; and that as between Mr. Chase and himself, the only differences that had occurred were mostly those which originated from questions of expediency.

I asked the President if he had sent for Senator Pomeroy. He replied that several persons had urged him to do so, but he had not complied with their suggestions; and that I might therefore infer that the Senator had called of his own accord; that Mr. Pomeroy had spoken in a very friendly manner, and on retiring had said that he would be pleased to receive from the President any suggestions that might tend toward producing a good effect in the present condition of affairs.

[72] Moses N. Wisewell of New Jersey, brevet brigadier-general of volunteers.
[73] Senator from Maryland 1845–1849, 1863–1868.

The President and his counsel are again together this morning, the answer being still under consideration.

The President attended the funeral of Wm. Slade, his Steward, this afternoon, at two o'clock, but the lawyers remained in consultation until 4:30 P. M.

Referring to the Philadelphia Convention[74] to-day, the President remarked that had it received the support of the Democracy, the new party would have been a success, and that he could perceive all along the object of certain party leaders, which was to use him as they would an orange.

March 19, 1868.

The President's counsel again in session. Mr. Groesbeck present to-day, as on yesterday.

March 20, 1868.

The President is not satisfied with the answer to the XIth article[75] prepared by Mr. Evarts. He therefore contemplates bringing before his counsel today his various messages, to show that they contain as strong charges against Congress officially as are made in any of the speeches he has delivered as a private citizen. He is not willing to take back any thing he has said, but expresses himself gratified at the opportunity of once again placing before the people the speeches made during the western tour.

Saturday, March 21, 1868.

The President was engaged with his lawyers today from one o'clock until five. Present, Messrs. Stanbery, Curtis, Evarts, Groesbeck and Nelson: Judge Black absent. As far as I can understand, he has become "miffed" about something that occurred day before yesterday, and has not been present since.[76] About three the counsel were invited into the Library to partake of refreshments. They laughed at the idea that anything could be made of the President's speeches, and did not seem to entertain any doubt of his acquittal.

Sunday, March 22, 1868.

The President's counsel met at 1.30 P.M. and had under consideration the answers to the Xth. and XIth. articles.[77] Present: Messrs. Stanbery, Curtis, Evarts, Groesbeck, and Nelson—Judge Black being again absent. The consultation was prolonged until five o'clock.

The President entertained some idea of appearing before the Senate in person tomorrow. He submitted the question to his lawyers, who were unanimous in the opinion that he should not attend in person.

The trouble between the President and Judge Black grew out of the Alta Vela case. The President seems to think that the Judge attempted to take advantage of the present condition of affairs to press a favorable consideration of that claim. The Judge and his son have recalled their acceptance of an invitation to dine with the President on Friday.

Monday, March 23d, 1868.

Attended the impeachment trial today, as a witness.[78]

[74] The National Union Convention of August 14, 1866.

[75] The article accusing Johnson of declaring the Thirty-Ninth Congress to be no congress, etc.

[76] See *post* p. 128, and Dewitt, *The Impeachment and Trial of Andrew Johnson*, pp. 373–400.

[77] The tenth article related to Johnson's intemperate speeches.

[78] Colonel Moore did not in fact testify until April 3.

March 24, 1868.

Counsel present until 12:25 P.M., when the Cabinet session commenced.

The President explained to me the cause of Judge Black's withdrawal as one of his counsel, remarking, " Because I did not consent to send a vessel of war to Alta Vela to oust one set of Americans in favor of another, and thereby produce a collision with the Dominican Republic, Judge Black refuses to act as my counsel. He has made a pretty record—one which will do him far more injury than it can me."

The President said that there had been some efforts made to heal the breach, and he had been urged by some, who he thought might be in the interest of the Judge, to send for that gentleman. This, the President declared, he would not do. He would rather be put to death than submit to such humiliation.

Wednesday, March 25, 1868.

The counsel again in session at the Executive Mansion.

The veto of the bill to withdraw from the Supreme Court the McCardle case submitted to the Senate.[79]

March 26, 1868.

The President and his counsel have been together all the afternoon. He thinks that after all his trouble with Judge Black may prove a godsend.

Friday, March 27, 1868.

The President discussed the propriety of placing Genl. Hancock in command of the Dept. of the East, or of the new Military Divn. of the Atlantic. He said the command of the latter had been offered to Sherman, a friend of Genl. Grant, and an officer somewhat in sympathy with Congress. Sherman having declined the command, the Presidt. thought it would be well now to offer it to Hancock. The difficulty, however, was whether the Head Qrs. should be at Philad., Baltimore, or Washington. There were good reasons, the President said, why they should be at either place—in Philad. because Hancock was a Pennsylvanian and was to relieve Genl. Meade, an officer from that State; at Baltimore, because that city was nearer Washington, and besides would serve somewhat to excite the apprehensions of men who cared not for law, and who were always pretending to fear an invasion from Maryland; at Washington, because ever since Mr. Stanton's removal the President had been kept in ignorance of the military preparations and precautions that had been going on, and he ought to have an officer in command here who could investigate what had been done, and inform him of all that transpired. At any rate (he continued) the order should be issued before Monday, the day set for trial, as its effect might be good.

As to placing Hancock in Meade's place, the President did not seem to care what Meade would think. The President said he had it from excellent authority that at the close of the war, when Grant's success had caused him to be named for the Presidency, Meade had asked the General that, in the event he should be elected to that position, to confer upon him a foreign mission. Meade, when on his way to Georgia, had not found time to call on him, (the President,) and yet he had been informed by the Person to whom he referred that that officer had made it convenient to call on General Grant, and again remind him of his wish to be appointed to a foreign mission, in the event of the General's elevation to the Presidency.

[79] A *habeas corpus* case involving the constitutionality of the reconstruction acts. *Dewitt,* p. 403.

March 27, 1868.

Have prepared an order relieving Hancock from the command of the Fifth Military District and assigning him to the command of the Military Division of the Atlantic.

The President said this morning, in referring to the suggestion that he should make some efforts to influence the impeachment trial: " I had rather be convicted ·than resort to fraud, corruption, or bribery of any kind—Conviction with a clear conscience is far, far preferable to acquittal, with a knowledge of guilt."

Speaking of Hancock, the President did not know but that after all New York would be the best place for the General's headquarters. There was a great focal power there, and besides he thought it would be consonant with Hancock's wishes. He thought that Hancock deeply felt the slight that Grant had attempted to put upon him in New Orleans, and had shown his manliness by refusing to exhibit the least cringing. " Mentally and physically " (said the President), " they were made in different moulds. General Grant, in the opinion of the people, is not a fair representative of the nation, mentally, morally, or physically. The people should have seen his attitude and looks as he withdrew from the Cabinet meeting the day his duplicity was exposed. The Goddess of History should have been present, to inscribe the scene upon her tablets. It would have shown Gen. Grant in his true colors. Lee will go down in history as a greater man than Grant. Grant was a mere figure-head, who by fortuitous circumstances won a reputation far above his real deserts."

The President told me that he had heard that Judge Black regretted his course in reference to the Alta Vela matter.

Saturday, March 28, 1868.

The President is much pleased with Hancock's letter to Governor Pease, of Texas, published in the Intelligencer of this morning.[80] Beginning with the Sentence, " When a boy, I remember to have read a speech of Lord Chatham delivered in Parliament," the President read the letter through and commented upon it, saying that it showed that General Hancock was governed by principles with which he had been imbued in youth, which he had not lost sight of, and which he could now bring into play. The letter was a platform upon which he (the President) would be willing to go before the country, and was upon the same line as the General's order upon assuming command of the 5th Military District. In his (the President's) opinion, it indicated more with respect to the principles of our Government than was ever in Genl. Grant's mind.

Informed the President, upon my return from the Capitol, of a rumor that in the High Court of Impeachment the Chief Justice would insist upon it, as a right, to decide questions of law. The President replied that he had been informed that the Justices of the Supreme Court had held a consultation upon the subject, and had concluded that

[80] This letter, dated March 9, 1868, and printed in the *National Intelligencer* of March 28, can be found reprinted in F. E. Goodrich's *Life of Hancock*, pp. 287–299, and in *The Civil Record of Hancock during his Administration in Louisiana and Texas*, pp. 6–14. The civil governor of Texas had urged Hancock to order a military commission for judicial purposes, but Hancock maintained that conditions in Texas were not sufficiently different from those in other states to warrant such a course, and asserted with vigor the propriety of coming back as soon as possible to the ordinary processes of civil justice.

the Chief Justice would have the right to determine all such questions. In this connection the President exhibited to me an anonymous note, written upon delicate, scented paper, in a masculine hand, to the following effect: "Let your counsel move to quash the indictment, the Chief Justice determine in its favor, and close the proceedings of the High Court. It will cause them to terminate to the confusion of your enemies."

Sunday, March 29, 1868.

The President went to hear Father Maguire this morning at St. Patrick's Church, and returned much pleased with the sermon. In the afternoon he refd. to the remarks of the Revd. Father, saying that in his sermon the preacher had alluded to the contest between the aristocracy and the poor. "Now" (said the President) "I don't know anything more depressing than for a man to labor for the people and not be understood. It is enough to sour his very soul. He may have nothing else at heart than the interests of the masses; he may struggle for their elevation; he may have nothing selfish in view, neither his own nor his relations' aggrandizement; and yet he may be deserted by the very persons in whose behalf he has given all that he has. Look at the Gracchi. They were accused of agrarianism; but as I understand it, their idea was to divide the lands that had been conquered, and which had been taken possession of by the nobility, among the people. They fell at the hands of the aristocracy. This American Senate is as corrupt as was then the Roman Senate, and you can place no more dependence in them when the interests of the people are concerned."

March 30, 1868.

The President was again strongly inclined to attend the Senate in person today, and was anxious for the appearance of his counsel. They presently came, and the President, returning to the Library, told me that he had concluded not to go to the Capitol.

March 31, 1868.—(Tuesday)

Cabinet meeting was held today, as usual on Tuesdays. One was also convened this evening, at eight o'clock, upon the request of the counsel.

After the adjournment of the afternoon session of the Cabinet, the President referred to the clause of the Constitution, that "Congress may by law provide for the case of removal, death, resignation, or inability both of the President and Vice President, declaring what officer shall then act as President," etc. He thought the Courts had already determined that a member of Congress was *not* an officer of the Government, and that in the event of his own removal from the Presidency it was doubtful whether Mr. Wade would be eligible for the succession.

April 1, 1868.

An act to exempt certain manufactures from internal taxes and for other purposes was submitted last evening for the President's approval. He signed it, but directly afterwards caused his approval to be erased, and requested me to take the bill to the Secretary of the Treasury and ask his opinion respecting its provisions. I did so; when the Secretary advised the approval of the bill, remarking that it was the first step towards a reduction of taxes, and that although it was only to benefit a class, and would reduce the revenue, it was estimated, about sixty millions, it contained provisions designed to facilitate the collection of the whiskey tax. Altogether, he thought the President would do well to sign the bill. Mr. Rollins, Commr. of Internal Revenue, who happened to be present, concurred in the Secretary's recommendation. I also consulted Honble. Edmund Cooper, who came to the same conclusion although expressing himself averse to such class legislation.

Saturday, April 4, 1868.

The President, this evening, spoke very freely of Genl. Grant, saying that he seemed to be daily growing guiltier in the public estimation, and that the time would yet come when he would be held in contempt by the people.

The President also .refd. to a double-leaded article in the N. Y. Tribune, viz: " We have assurance from Washington that Genl. Grant finds it not inconsistent with his duty as a soldier to announce it as his opinion that the only hope for the peace of the country is the success of the pending impeachment trial. He feels that the national security demands the removal of the President. If the trial should fail, the people can only expect more assumptions of power, and a more determined resistance to law. When the General of our armies entertains this conviction, there is no room for doubt as to the duty of the Senate. The loyal nation demands the President's removal."

" What an idea," said the President, " that the opinion of the General of the army should serve as a guide for the Senate in a matter of impeachment! Is it not another indication that the purpose of the Radicals is a military despotism? What a few years since would have been the fate of the General commanding the military forces if he had done what the Tribune, with such an air of authority, says Genl. Grant has done?" The President was inclined to doubt the accuracy of the Tribune's statement, on the ground that the General could hardly have been so indiscreet as thus to express himself.

Monday, April 6, 1868.

The President divides into three classes those who are now opposing him, viz: 1st. Those who desire his removal because he is an obstacle to their partisan and unconstitutional designs. 2d. Those who, although not widely, if at all differing from him in political opinions, have failed in their efforts to control him, and make him a mere instrument in their hands. 3d. Those who have a grudge against him for the part he took during the war.

April 7, 1868.

The President is very indignant at a letter of " Mac ", in the Cincinnati Commercial of the 3d, purporting to give a conversation between the President and himself. It was (the President said) an outrage upon him, and was not a truthful statement of the interview. He repeated what he had said to " Mac " respecting Adjt. Genl. Thomas, viz. that the General had made a great mistake, when he first called upon the Secretary of War with an ad interim appointment, in not at once taking possession of the War Dept.; that being of a chivalric disposition, the General had placed too much reliance in what Mr. Stanton had said to him; and that he doubtless felt that he could not, without violence to his gentlemanly feelings, refuse Mr. Stanton's request for time to remove his papers. Genl. Thomas of course felt elated by' his appointment, and had given utterance to remarks which were very indiscreet. The President admitted that he had committed an error in selecting the General, whom, however, he believed to be an honorable, straightforward man.

April 8, 1868.

The President declares that the defence he desires to make in the impeachment trial is for the people—not merely for the Senate, and that he would care nothing for conviction by that body if he stands acquitted by the nation.

CPSIA information can be obtained
at www.ICGtesting.com
Printed in the USA
BVHW071635280119
538842BV00033B/3507/P

9 781333 689407